Please Don't Sneeze!

A traditional tale

One day, Wild Dog was
walking along a path
in the jungle. He found
a large bone lying
on the ground.

"This is my lucky day,"
he said. He picked the bone
up and went on his way.

The bone was so big
that Wild Dog
couldn't see where
he was going.

Suddenly, he fell into
a great big pit in
the middle of the path.

The pit was so deep
that Wild Dog could
not jump out. He sat
down and thought for
a while. Then he
decided on a
clever plan.

Soon, Wild Pig came along
and looked down into
the pit.

"Why are you down there,
Wild Dog?" he asked.

"Lion is hungry today, and this is a special hiding place where I will be safe," answered Wild Dog.

"I'd better come and hide with you!" said Wild Pig.

"But you might sneeze, and if Lion hears you he'll know where we are," said Wild Dog. "So...
Please don't wheeze.
Please don't sneeze.
I ask you kindly,
please, please, please!"

"I won't wheeze *or* sneeze!" promised Wild Pig, and he jumped down into the pit.

Before long, Wild Horse came by and saw Wild Dog and Wild Pig down in the pit.

"Why are you down there?" she asked.

Then Wild Dog told
Wild Horse what he
had told Wild Pig.
*"Please don't wheeze.
Please don't sneeze.
I ask you kindly,
please, please, please!"*

Now Wild Horse wanted
to hide as well.

"I promise that I won't
wheeze *or* sneeze,"
she said, and she jumped
down into the pit.

Next, Elephant came along, and the same thing happened. Wild Dog sang his little song.

"Please don't wheeze.
Please don't sneeze.
I ask you kindly,
please, please, please!"

It was now getting crowded in the pit.

Wild Dog looked around at the other animals.

"Are you sure you're not going to sneeze?" he asked. "We *must* keep our hiding place secret!"

"No!" said Wild Pig, Wild Horse, and Elephant. "We won't sneeze!"

21

Suddenly, Wild Dog took
a deep breath and sneezed
the most enormous sneeze
the other animals
had ever heard.

"AH-CHOOOOOOOO!"

"Oh no!" cried Wild Pig and Wild Horse. "Shhh! Lion will hear you!"

Wild Dog sneezed again, and Elephant tossed him right out of the pit.

Back on the jungle path,
Wild Dog barked goodbye
to the animals in the pit.
Then he went happily
on his way!